ACKNOWLEDGMENTS

I have to thank numerous people who helped to make this book a reality. Without their help, this book would simply not exist.

To my Mom and Dad, who were not only the first people to teach me about Jesus, but who also tirelessly helped edit this book. To Justo Borrero, my illustrator, who created the beautiful and fun illustrations that brought the book to life. To my wife and kids (Lisa, Alexa, and John Otto) who love me enough to put up with my crazy ideas. To Rachel Hechter, who continues to provide amazing assistance with all of my writing. To three of the best pastors on earth who helped me learn that pastors could be real men leading churches full of real people: Matt Mills, Jon Ireland, and Todd Rodarmel. To the rest of my friends and family who have shaped and supported my life for the past 42 years.

And finally to Jesus, without whom this book and this life wouldn't be nearly as good. :-)

— **John Rydell III**

Copyright © 2020 by Puppy Dogs & Ice Cream, Inc.
All rights reserved. Published in the United States
by Puppy Dogs & Ice Cream, Inc.
ISBN: 978-1-953177-55-1
Edition: December 2020

For all inquiries, please contact us at:
info@puppysmiles.org

To see more of our books, visit us at:
www.PuppyDogsAndIceCream.com

Bible Rhymes for Young Minds
The Life of Jesus

Written by John Rydell III
Illustrated by Justo Borrero

Oh, the world was so perfect when first it began,
But people messed up God's original plan.

For a very long time, God's people were lost,
And God wanted them back... no matter the cost.

So God spoke to Noah and Moses and others,
Abraham, David, and sisters, and brothers.

2

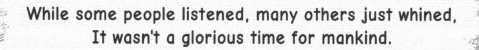

While some people listened, many others just whined,
It wasn't a glorious time for mankind.

Then God promised his people he'd send them a king,
A person so great that he'd fix everything.

We all needed someone to save us from sin,
And so this amazing old story begins.

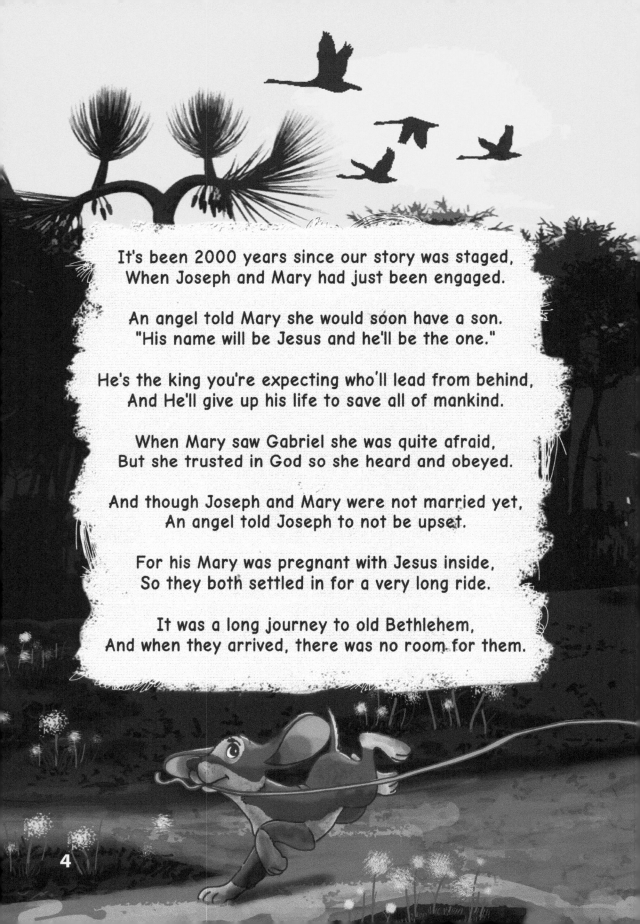

It's been 2000 years since our story was staged,
When Joseph and Mary had just been engaged.

An angel told Mary she would soon have a son.
"His name will be Jesus and he'll be the one."

He's the king you're expecting who'll lead from behind,
And He'll give up his life to save all of mankind.

When Mary saw Gabriel she was quite afraid,
But she trusted in God so she heard and obeyed.

And though Joseph and Mary were not married yet,
An angel told Joseph to not be upset.

For his Mary was pregnant with Jesus inside,
So they both settled in for a very long ride.

It was a long journey to old Bethlehem,
And when they arrived, there was no room for them.

In a manger of hay, our sweet Jesus was born.
Mary wrapped Him in rags, bits of cloth that were torn.

Then an angel appeared to some shepherds that night,
And he spoke of a king who'd been born with delight.

They visited Jesus and confirmed all the clues,
And went out in the world to spread the good news.

When King Herod heard Jesus was laid in a manger,
He ordered three wise men to check out the danger.

They followed a star in the far eastern sky,
The king seemed so scared that they had to know why.

Of His first 30 years, there is little we know,
As a worker of wood, He continued to grow.

A great prophet named John preached abroad in that day.
It was his duty to prepare the way.

John lived near the Jordan, maybe in a tent.
He baptized the people and told them – repent.

Jesus was baptized and His journey began.
This was all part of God's wonderful plan.

When the Spirit descended in the form of a dove,
God told the world, "Here's my son whom I love!"

Nicodemus, a teacher, a powerful Jew,
Came to see Jesus to learn what to do.

In teaching the rules Nic was really a pro,
But the true love of God he sure didn't show.

If he wanted a closeness with God to begin,
He learned that he needed to be born again.

The tax man named Matthew was hated for real,
But one night he asked Jesus to join in a meal.

When the Pharisees saw this they got really mad,
Because Jesus was eating with men who were bad.

But Jesus was sent to the earth to save sinners,
His mission was not to the religious winners.

A Samaritan woman He met at a well.
She was shameful and scandalous, Jesus could tell.

A woman like her, folks were well-taught to hate,
But the love of Lord Jesus – it altered her fate.

She realized He was Messiah the King.
He'd give her new life through a fresh living spring.

The woman believed Him and told the whole town.
Her story helped Jesus to gain great renown.

Jesus loved everyone, the young and the old,
The rich and the poor, the meek and the bold.

Jesus was brave and He tore down old rules.
He told those in power to not be such fools.

Love your neighbors, He taught them. Just ask what they need.
And always remember to do only good deeds.

He healed all the people who had faith in Him,
And taught lots of people that life was not grim.

Everyone's welcome with Jesus you see.
It's the same for us all—both for you and for me.

Just tell Him your troubles and your acts of sin,
And your new life with Jesus will surely begin.

Our job here on earth is to live more like Jesus,
To strive to be like Him and learn what He teaches.

The crowds longed to hear what Lord Jesus would say,
So they followed Him up on a mountain one day.

The sermon He preached surprised some in the crowd,
For it was not meant for the rich or the proud.

Blessings upon blessings... oh, did He shower,
On the poor, sick and lame who hadn't much power.

The people who listened had learned many rules,
From the priests and the temples and religious schools.

But Jesus taught them that it would be smart
To love God and your neighbor with all of your heart.

He wanted their lives to be beacons for others,
Doing good things for both strangers and brothers.

Then Jesus taught them how to pray:
Our Father God in Heaven today,

Please help us do the things you say
And let the earth be run your way.

Forgive us for the bad we do
And we'll forgive our enemies too.

Give us daily food to nourish
And the inner strength to flourish.

Give us strength to stay away
From evil things that come our way.

You deserve amazing glory
For your never-ending story.

Pharisees taught them that men should not kill,
But loving your enemy was Jesus' will.

Prayer and good deeds you should not do to brag,
Because when you do, you make people gag.

Don't fall in love with your stuff or your money.
For self-absorbed people are not kind or funny.

Do not live a life that's too hectic and hurried,
Nor spend too much time in your life being worried.

People's mistakes you should try not to judge,
And never--not ever--should you hold a grudge.

Say a prayer to your God for the things that you need,
But don't say a prayer that is based on your greed.

The things Jesus told us were not just for thought.
So go out and do all the things He has taught.

Jesus healed many people and cured mental strife.
And those who had faith got to live a new life.

A man had a son with a demon and seizures,
But Lord Jesus cured him in front of believers.

Two men came to Jesus because they were blind.
They were filled with great faith that He would be kind.

Jesus touched their sad eyes, and then they had sight.
Because of their faith, they now saw the light.

20

A man who had leprosy knelt before Jesus,
And begged the Lord Savior to cure his diseases.

Sick people like him had to live all alone,
But once Jesus cured him he was free to go home.

A poor troubled woman had been sick for 12 years.
She'd spent all her money and been driven to tears.

One day in a crowd, she touched Jesus' robe.
A miracle happened, now told over the globe.

21

Jesus taught lessons both caring and bold.
Here are just some of the stories He told:

God's words are like seeds that need soil to grow,
If you listen and hear them His love you will know.

Believing in Jesus is like mustard's small seed.
Its growth is so large your best dreams you'll exceed.

A man will sell all for a field with great treasure,
But sharing your stuff will give Jesus great pleasure.

A servant did not have to pay back his loan.
The joy of forgiveness is what has been shown.

A Samaritan stopped to help a hurt man.
If we do the same we will follow God's plan.

It should not make you mad when it's your turn to labor,
To show love and care for your friends and your neighbors.

Just like a good shepherd whose poor sheep are lost,
Jesus will find you no matter the cost.

A man threw a party but nobody came,
So instead he invited the poor, sick and lame.

The things you are good at are God's gifts to you,
So using your talents is what you should do.

Now Jesus was known for the stories He told.
The lessons He taught had more value than gold.

A boy went to his father and asked for some cash.
He gave his son money, even though he was brash.

The son moved away and did many bad things.
He blew all the money on scandalous flings.

But when he went home and confessed to his dad,
His father forgave him and was not at all mad.

Say you're sorry to God for bad deeds you've done.
And He'll welcome you back like His very own son.

Jesus slept on a boat near the old Galilee,
When suddenly there was a storm on the sea.

Jesus awoke, told His disciples to chill,
Then commanded the sea to have peace and be still.

His disciples perceived that He might be the one,
Based on the miracles that He had done.

The disciples were back on the boat for the night,
When they all beheld a miraculous sight.

They got super scared just like we would be,
When Jesus came walking on top of the sea.

Jesus sent the apostles to use their new skills,
To heal the sick and the lame of all of their ills.

They healed and they taught as they went town to town.
They trusted in God and did good with no frown.

When they returned from their trip, they sat down on a lawn.
And Jesus asked how their long travels had gone.

5,000 people had come to see Jesus,
And said to themselves, "What more can He teach us?"

But the people got hungry and had to be fed.
So Jesus fed all with two fish and some bread.

29

There were too many rules about keeping things clean.
Those who made up these rules were judgmental and mean.

Jesus said "It's not just about the foods that you eat."
What matters is when you lie, steal, and cheat.

One morning the Pharisees brought Christ a lady.
She had been caught doing something quite shady.

They all hoped that Jesus would punish the fact
That the woman committed a very bad act.

Then Jesus ensured that no rocks would be thrown.
"A person who's sinless should throw the first stone."

So Jesus taught how to forgive human sin,
Which made all the Pharisees madder at him.

He said He had come here to do His God's work,
But some didn't believe Him and called Him a jerk.

The Pharisees hated the power He had,
And decided to kill Him because they were mad.

When Jesus' friend Lazarus got sick and died,
On that very sad day the Lord Jesus, He cried.

Four very long days, Laz in his tomb laid,
When Jesus looked up to His God and then prayed.

"Hey Laz! Come on out of the tomb," Jesus said,
And instantly Laz was then raised from the dead.

Then Jesus began to speak of His reign.
He told of the kingdom that they could obtain.

"The kingdom of God isn't just for the wealthy."
"Nor is it just for the strong and the healthy."

"I am the redeemer and life you will see."
"You will never die when you have faith in me."

Jesus told His disciples that He was the Christ,
That His end was near and He'd be sacrificed.

In order to bring true forgiveness for men,
He was going to die and be raised up again.

Jesus was friendly with someone named Mary,
Who realized the burden He soon was to carry.

So Mary used perfume whose smell was so sweet
To wash all the dirt off of Jesus' feet.

She loved her Lord Jesus whom she lavished with care.
She wept and then cleaned Him with all of her hair.

He came to Jerusalem—just one week to go.
He rode on the back of a donkey real slow.

Lots of people loved Jesus...kids, dads and moms.
So they covered his path with their clothes and some palms.

Like a triumphant king, he returned to this town.
The people all cheered and they didn't dare frown.

But they didn't know he was a new kind of king.
And that heaven on earth he was coming to bring.

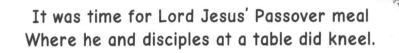

It was time for Lord Jesus' Passover meal
Where he and disciples at a table did kneel.

Right before dinner, with water and a sheet
He went to each one of them, washing their feet.

He taught them the love of a humble, wise pastor
When showing them he was a servant--not master.

"I'll never desert you," a brash Peter chimes.
But then Jesus says, "You'll deny me three times."

"Do the following things in remembrance of me,
And the love of Christ Jesus all people will see."

He held up some bread and said "This you should do."
The body of Christ which is broken for you.

Then after the dinner he gave them some wine,
And told them that this was to be a new sign.

The blood on the cross he was going to shed,
So they would not die but have new life instead.

I am going to God so rejoice and be glad!
It's a time for great joy, not a time to be sad.

Jesus said he would send them his Spirit – a helper,
To give them support and a lifetime of shelter.

The time was approaching, the hour had come
For God, Jesus' father, to exalt his own son.

When the sun went down at the end of the day,
Jesus went to the garden to sit down and pray.

Despite all of his knowledge and lessons he'd taught,
Jesus the man was extremely distraught.

Jesus wanted his friends to be with him and pray.
But instead they had fallen asleep for the day.

His disciple called Judas did something so grim,
When he told the Sanhedrin just where to find him.

The Sanhedrin sent guards to do a deed quite vile,
To arrest the Lord Jesus and put him on trial.

To the Governor Pilate the soldiers did bring,
The man named Jesus who said He was king.

Jesus said to the people, "You know who I am.
I have nothing to hide – this trial's a sham."

A convict, Barabbas, had just killed a man,
Which gave Pontius Pilate an idea for a plan.

He asked the big crowd who should die on that day.
Jesus or Barabbas – which one should he slay?

Pilate thought Jesus had done nothing wrong,
But people yelled "Kill Him" and Pilate went along.

So the soldiers and Romans mocked Him eye to eye,
Robed Him in purple and sent Him to die.

The Roman centurions were told by their boss
To go and nail Jesus upon an old cross.

Two other criminals were hanged next to Him.
The whole situation was so sad and grim.

Being nailed to a cross was the worst way to die.
To His mom and His friends, Jesus murmured goodbye.

Although all the soldiers mocked Him and made fun,
Lord Jesus forgave them for what they had done.

Jesus hanged on the cross for six hours of pain,
But this lamb of God would not die here in vain.

He raised His eyes upward and prayed from the tree:
"Father, my God, will you take care of me?"

When Jesus took in His last breath and then died,
The people were filled with such grief that they cried.

An earthquake occurred and the sky turned dark gray,
The scared and young soldiers just ran right away.

For three days Lord Jesus was in the tomb dead,
Wrapped up in a sheet from His toes to His head.

Mary went to the tomb one glorious day.
The rock marking the tomb had been rolled right away!

An angel then told her "Don't worry, just listen.
Jesus has overcome death and has risen!"

Word started to spread of the wonderful news,
That He was alive now, the king of the Jews!

We celebrate Easter to remember the day,
He saved us from sin this miraculous way.

Jesus was shown as Messiah and King,
And that the new kingdom of God He would bring.

Oh... The risen Lord Jesus appeared all around,
Near the sea, on the roads, and in many a town.

He met with friend Peter alone on a beach
For something important He still had to teach.

He comforted Peter and said don't be grim,
And 3 times He said that He loved and forgave him.

He told Peter to build a great church and do things
That would impact the world even more than good kings.

One day 10 disciples were in a room waiting.
The death of Lord Jesus they still were debating.

When all of a sudden Lord Jesus showed up.
He showed them His scars and then drank from a cup.

Then they all knew with certainty it was no lie.
The Lord Jesus had risen and no more would die.

A disciple named Thomas thought all might be lies,
Until he saw Jesus with his very own eyes.

Then Jesus said something important you see –
"Blessed are those who believe without seeing me."

40 days passed since he'd been raised from the dead.
To the top of Mount Olives the disciples He led.

He showed His great glory to His favorite eleven.
They bowed and they praised as He lifted to heaven.

In a glorious act Jesus lifted both hands,
And to His disciples came His final command.

He told His disciples to spread the good news,
To all the world's people, both gentiles and Jews.

Heal all of God's children – the poor, sick and lame,
Baptizing everyone in Lord Jesus' name.

The Spirit of God then descended on them,
To dwell with His people forever. Amen.

CPSIA information can be obtained
at www.ICGtesting.com
Printed in the USA
BVHW012134091222
653892BV00028B/415